INTRODUCTION

Turtles lay eggs—and you get turtles. Alligators lay eggs—and you get alligators. But butterflies lay eggs— and what do you get? Caterpillars!

The life cycle of a butterfly is truly amazing. A tiny egg hatches and a caterpillar crawls out. The caterpillar eats and grows. Then it disappears into a case called a chrysalis. After a while a stunning butterfly emerges. Away it flies.

Where Did the Butterfly Get Its Name? traces the lives of butterflies and moths from egg to caterpillar, to chrysalis or cocoon, to adult. But this book does much, much more. It answers dozens of questions about butterflies and moths. It tells you the differences between them. It discusses the foods they eat and the enemies that eat them. And it looks at the many ways butterflies and moths escape their enemies.

Have you ever wondered:

- Do butterflies sit on their eggs?
- Can butterflies and moths walk?
- Do moths chew their food?
- Why do moths fly around lights?

Wonder no longer. Read on and find out all you want to know about the incredible butterflies and moths!

Melvin Berger   Gilda Berger

ALL IN THE FAMILY

Where did the butterfly get its name?

Most likely from some old ideas about butterflies. People used to believe that butterflies flew into kitchens, attracted by butter and milk. Some say that's why the German word for butterfly is *milchdieb*, which means "milk thief."

   Other people say the name comes from the Old English word *buterflëoge*, meaning "butter" and "flying creature." This probably refers to the yellow color of many butterflies.

Who named the moth?

The moth also got its name from Old English. In this language, the word for moth is *moththe*.

Are butterflies and moths the same?

No. But they are alike in many ways. Butterflies and moths are both insects. And like all insects, they have three main body parts: head, thorax, and abdomen. They also have six legs, two pairs of wings, two big eyes, two antennae or feelers, and a long, thin, coiled feeding tube called a proboscis (pro-BAHS-is). The wings and legs are connected to the thorax.

Do butterflies and moths have a heart?

Yes. The butterfly or moth heart is in the thorax. The heart pumps blood through the animal's body, just as it does in humans. But, believe it or not, the blood of a butterfly or a moth is yellow, green, or colorless. It's never red.

WHERE DID THE BUTTERFLY GET ITS NAME?

Questions and Answers About Butterflies and Moths

BY MELVIN AND GILDA BERGER
ILLUSTRATED BY HIGGINS BOND

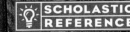

SCHOLASTIC REFERENCE

CONTENTS

KEY TO ABBREVIATIONS
cm = centimeter/centimetre
g = gram
km = kilometer/kilometre
kph = kilometers/kilometres per hour
m = meter/metre
°C = degrees Celsius

Library of Congress Cataloging-in-Publication Data

Berger, Melvin
    Where Did the Butterfly Get Its Name? : questions and answers about butterflies and moths/by
    Melvin and Gilda Berger ; illustrated by Higgins Bond.
        p. cm. -- (Scholastic question and answer series)
    Summary: Presents information about the physical characteristics, habitat, behavior, and life cycle of
    butterflies and moths in question-and-answer format.
    1. Butterflies--Miscellanea--Juvenile literature. 2. Moths--Miscellanea--Juvenile literature. [1.
    Butterflies--Miscellanea. 2. Moths--Miscellanea. 3. Questions and answers.] I. Berger, Gilda. II. Bond,
    Higgins, ill. III. Title.

QE544.2 .B475 2003   595.78--dc21   2001042642
ISBN 0-439-26675-0

Book design by David Saylor and Nancy Sabato

10 9 8 7 6 5 4 3   04 05 06 07
                                   08
Printed in the U.S.A.
First trade printing, March 2003

Expert reader: Leslie T. Sharpe
Naturalist
Fire Island Ecology Coalition
New York, NY

The insects on the cover are tiger swallowtail butterflies. White-lined sphinx moths are on the title page.
The caterpillar on page 3 is a robin moth caterpillar.

To Nancy and Mitch, bright and colorful
—M. and G. Berger

To my wonderful grandmother, Pearlee Willis, whose
flower gardens attracted the most beautiful butterflies
—Higgins Bond

Robin moth

American painted
lady butterfly

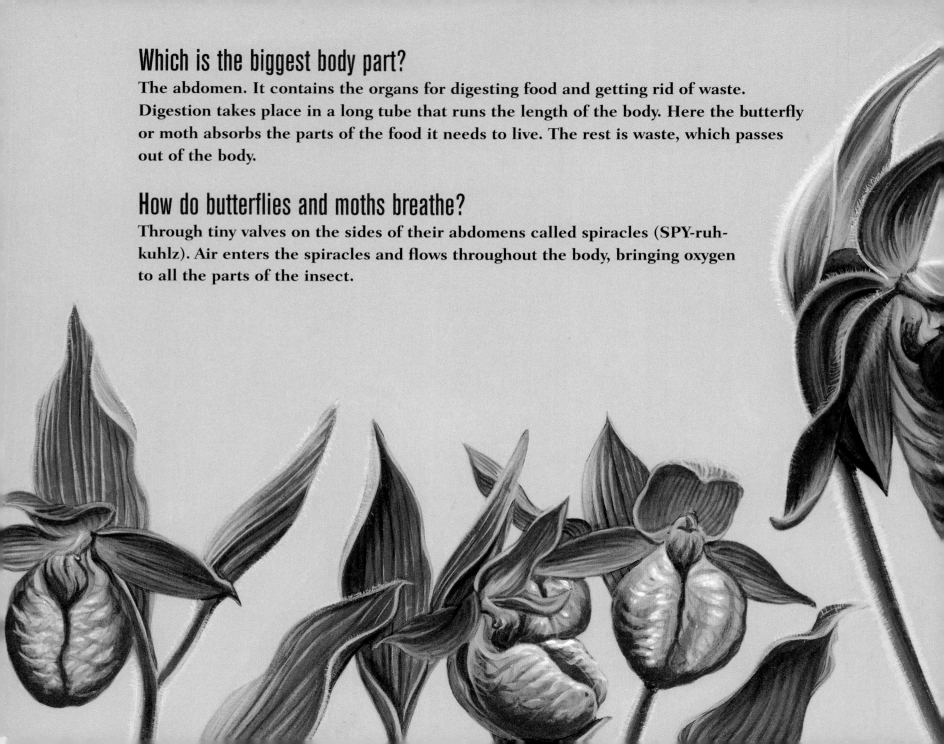

Which is the biggest body part?

The abdomen. It contains the organs for digesting food and getting rid of waste. Digestion takes place in a long tube that runs the length of the body. Here the butterfly or moth absorbs the parts of the food it needs to live. The rest is waste, which passes out of the body.

How do butterflies and moths breathe?

Through tiny valves on the sides of their abdomens called spiracles (SPY-ruh-kuhlz). Air enters the spiracles and flows throughout the body, bringing oxygen to all the parts of the insect.

Do butterflies and moths have bones?

No, they don't. Like other insects, however, they do have stiff outside skeletons, called exoskeletons.

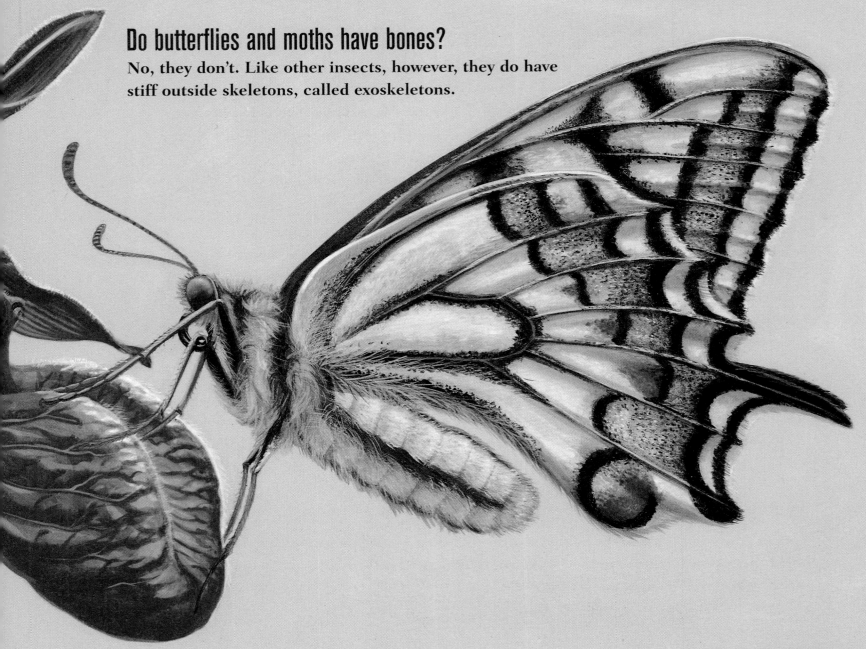

Common yellow swallowtail butterfly

How many kinds of butterflies and moths are there?

So far, scientists have counted about 20,000 different kinds of butterflies. But they have found an amazing 140,000 kinds of moths!

Together, butterflies and moths make up a group of insects known as *Lepidoptera* (lep-ih-DOP-ter-uh). The name comes from the Greek words for "scale," since their wings are covered with thousands of tiny scales, and for "wing."

Become an expert on butterflies and moths and you'll be a lepidopterist!

How many wings do *Lepidoptera* have?

Four. There are a pair of front wings and a pair of back wings. The wings are thin, clear sheets of tissue. Inside are little, dark, stiff rods called veins. The veins work like the wooden or plastic rods in kites. They stiffen the wings and keep them at the right angle for flying. The veins also help make designs on the wings.

What are the scales for?

To give the wings color. The scales are actually tiny. They are many different colors. Look closely through a magnifier. You'll see the scales overlapping, like tiles on a roof.

Even the brightest butterflies and moths have some dark or black scales on their wings. These scales soak up sunlight and help keep the insects warm.

What is the powder on your fingers after you touch a butterfly or a moth?

Lots of tiny wing scales. The scales scatter like dust when you touch them. That's why it's best to leave butterflies and moths alone. Touching a butterfly or moth wing means the insect may never fly again and it may die.

Small tortoiseshell butterfly

Very close-up view of scales

Close-up view of scales

Both the moth and the butterfly are drawn one-half size.

Queen Alexandria
birdwing butterfly

Hercules moth

1   2   3   4   5   6   7   8

Do any butterflies and moths have few scales?

Yes. Those with see-through wings. These butterflies and moths are nearly invisible. The glasswing butterfly is a good example. It lives deep in the Amazonian jungle, where it flies close to the ground—and is very hard to see.

The unusual bee moth from Sri Lanka also has see-through wings. It looks just like a bee, and even flies like a bee, but it is not a bee. It is a moth.

Are all *Lepidoptera* wings the same shape?

No. Wings can be nearly round, triangular, square, or have "tails" sticking out in back. The insect's flying pattern depends on its wing shape.

Generally, butterflies and moths with large, wide wings flutter around in circles. You may have seen viceroys flitting about in a field or garden. Those with long, thin wings usually fly fast and straight. The death's-head hawkmoth is one of the fastest-flying moths. Its backward-pointed wings look like those of a jet fighter plane.

Which butterfly has the biggest wings?

The Queen Alexandria birdwing from New Guinea. The wings of this giant butterfly can be 11 inches (28 cm) across. That's about as big as a dinner plate!

The smallest butterfly is the pygmy blue. This pretty little insect is as small as ⅜ inch (1 cm) across!

Which moth has the biggest wings?

The giant Hercules moth of Australia. This moth is even bigger than the Queen Alexandria birdwing butterfly. When open, the wings of the Hercules moth are as long as a ruler—1 foot (30 cm) from tip to tip.

The leaf miner moth takes the prize as the smallest moth. Its outstretched wings measure only ⅛ inch (0.3 cm) wide.

Are all butterflies and moths colorful?

No. Butterflies are usually colorful. But most moths are brown or gray.

Most butterflies are bright because they fly by day. Their colorful wings make them hard to see among the flowers. At night, they hide on stems and leaves, or in dark places where birds and bats can't find them.

Moths usually fly by night. Their dull wings help them blend into the darkness. They are hard to spot during the day, too, as they rest on walls, fences, or tree trunks.

How fast do butterflies and moths fly?

Very fast. The fastest fliers beat their wings as often as 600 times a minute. A frightened butterfly or moth can reach speeds of 30 miles an hour (48.3 kph).

Do butterflies fly on cloudy days?

Not usually. Clouds may tell butterflies that a storm is coming. Also, clouds hide the sun, which butterflies may use to find their way. Without the sun to guide them, butterflies may become confused and lost.

How do moths find their way in the dark?

They use the moon to guide them. In fact, that explains why moths flit around streetlights and house lights at night. The moths probably confuse these lights with glimmers from the moon. The habit of flying around lights is bad for moths. It makes them easy targets for night-flying bats.

Are there any wingless moths?

Yes, a few. The female winter moth, for example, has no wings. She lives only one winter. The moth spends the entire time crawling around the plant on which she was born.

Luna moth

Why do resting butterflies or moths sometimes shake their wings?

To warm up. The best temperature for butterflies and moths to fly is about 86 degrees Fahrenheit (30° C). They must first warm up their muscles. They do this by shaking their wings or by basking in the sun. Then, it's up, up, and away!

How can you tell a butterfly from a moth when it is at rest?

By the angle of its wings. Butterflies usually rest with their wings touching, straight up over their bodies. Most resting moths, on the other hand, slide their wings flat over each other. The front pair of wings covers part of the back wings.

Large copper butterfly

How can you tell a butterfly from a moth when it is flying?

By its antennae and body shape. Moths tend to be smaller and plumper than butterflies. That is because moths fly at night when there is no sun to warm them. Their heavier bodies help hold in body heat.

Butterfly antennae are usually long and thin, with little knobs, or clubs, on the ends. Almost all moth antennae have no knobs. They look more feathery.

What are antennae used for?

Smelling, mostly. Each antenna has thousands of tiny holes that pick up odors. The antennae help butterflies and moths find food and locate their mates.

The females give off a special scent that the males smell with their antennae. A male emperor moth holds the record as the sharpest smeller. This moth can sniff out a female from 7 miles (11.3 km) away!

Oleander hawkmoth

Why does one butterfly or moth fly around another one?

To pick up the other's smell. The butterflies and moths release special body odors, called pheromones (FER-oh-mohnz). If the smell is right, the male and female mate.

The female vapourer moth has a big problem. She only has short wings and cannot fly. So she must attract males to her. When ready to mate, she rests on a tree trunk and pumps out smells. Any male flying nearby picks up the scent and zips toward her.

Most moths and butterflies have short lives. In order to multiply, they need to mate and lay eggs very quickly.

Why do moths touch their antennae with their legs?

To clean them. As moths feed, flower pollen piles up on their antennae. They use the stiff spines and hairs on their legs to brush away the pollen. Spotless antennae are best for picking up smells.

Can butterflies and moths walk?

Yes—but usually not very far or very well.

All insects have six legs. But not every kind of butterfly and moth walks on all six. Some have just four legs that are strong enough for walking. These butterflies and moths tuck the two weak legs under their heads to keep them out of the way.

How do butterflies and moths taste plants?

Mostly with their feet! The insects land on plants feet first. Each foot has a pair of tiny claws to grasp the plant. It also has hairy pads for tasting. As soon as the butterflies or moths touch down, they know if the plant is the right food for caterpillars and therefore a good place to lay eggs.

Small pearl-bordered fritillary

Passion vine butterfly

Pollen

What do butterflies and moths eat?

Liquids. Most butterflies and moths drink nectar, a sweet sugary liquid found inside flowers. But the purple emperor butterfly sips liquids it finds in the bodies of dead animals and in rotting fruits. Sometimes the juices contain so much alcohol that the butterfly gets drunk and can't fly!

Some kinds of moths drink only the fluids found in the eyes of cattle, deer, or elephants. Others mostly sip the liquids in animal droppings. But the Asian vampire moth is most unusual of all. It pierces the skin of cattle, pigs, and even elephants—and drinks their blood!

How does a butterfly or moth sip liquids?

With its proboscis, or feeding tube. Most of the time the proboscis is curled up like a coil. But when the insect is ready to eat, the proboscis unwinds. The long, thin tube works like a drinking straw. It reaches deep into the flower, fruit, or animal to suck up the liquid.

An African moth, the Darwin hawkmoth, has the longest proboscis of all. It stretches out to about 13 inches (35 cm)! That's three times the length of its body.

Do butterflies and moths chew their food?

No. Adult butterflies and moths only suck nectar and other liquids.

Do any moths live without eating?

Yes. The large Indian moon moth, for example, never takes in any food. It lives only a few days and survives on food stored up in its body. No wonder it has no proboscis!

Do butterflies and moths make sounds?

A few do. The cracker butterfly makes a clicking sound as it flies. The noise comes from the wings bumping into each other.

A death's-head hawkmoth produces a whistling sound as it forces air out of its throat. The wind rushing through a hollow tube in its wings allows a male whistling moth to make a sound.

The squeaks of a tiger moth protect it from bats that make similar sounds. The confused bats usually leave the tiger moths alone.

How do butterflies and moths hear?

Some kinds of butterflies and moths have "ears." These are tiny, flat circles on the sides of the thorax. These disks help the insects pick up many sounds, including the squeaks of nearby bats—the insects' worst enemy.

How do butterflies and moths see?

With two huge eyes. Each eye is made up of thousands of tiny eyes, which are really lenses. Each lens faces a slightly different direction. It forms a separate little picture of its surroundings. The insects' brain then puts all the pictures together and sees all around—especially the approach of an enemy. Just try creeping up on a butterfly or moth—and you'll see what we mean!

How well can butterflies and moths see?

Very well. Most can see objects up to 9 feet (2.7 m) away—farther than any other insect.

Do butterflies and moths have eyelids?

No. Their eyes are always open.

North American blue

Close-up view of eye

FROM EGG TO ADULT

Do newborn butterflies and moths look like their parents?

No. During their lifetimes all butterflies and moths pass through four stages: egg, caterpillar, pupa, and adult. Each stage looks very different. This process is called metamorphosis (*met*-uh-MOR-fuh-siss), a Greek word meaning "change in form."

A female butterfly or moth lays a number of tiny eggs. Each egg hatches and a caterpillar, or larva (the plural is larvae [LAR-vee]), crawls out. The caterpillar eats and eats. Eventually, most butterfly caterpillars form a chrysalis (KRIS-uh-lis); most moth caterpillars spin a cocoon. Inside, the caterpillar changes into a butterfly or into a moth. This is the pupa stage (the plural is pupae [PIU-pee]). Finally, the chrysalis or cocoon opens and a butterfly or moth comes out and flies away. The adults mate. And the life cycle starts again.

Where do butterflies and moths lay their eggs?

Mostly on the undersides of plant leaves or on stems. The female flits around "tasting" many plants. Finally, she finds one that will be food for the caterpillars when the eggs hatch. She lays the eggs and flies away.

How many eggs do butterflies and moths lay?

A few to several hundred. But not many eggs actually hatch. Too many animals, including birds and bats, find them a tasty treat.

What do the eggs look like?

They are very tiny. Most eggs are about the size of the head of a pin. The largest butterfly egg is no more than about ⅛ inch (0.3 cm) across.

The eggs are usually yellowish-white or light green. But over time, the colors may change to bright red or orange. Some eggs are flat ovals. Others are round with lines of darker colors around the sides.

As it grows, the caterpillar eats most of the inner part of the egg. This makes the eggshell so thin that you can see the inside. After a while, you can even make out the caterpillar's dark head within the shell.

Chalcedon checkerspot butterfly laying eggs

South American owl butterfly caterpillars

How long is it before the eggs hatch?

A few days to several weeks. But it can take longer if the butterfly lays its eggs near the end of summer. These caterpillars don't come out until late the following spring! Also, the eggs hatch sooner in warm weather than when it is cold.

How do the caterpillars get out of the eggs?

They bite the top off. The wormlike caterpillars then eat out a circle. Once the opening is big enough, the caterpillars wiggle and wriggle out of the eggs. The caterpillars work fast, since birds, frogs, spiders, lizards, and many other animals like to eat newly hatched caterpillars.

What happens to the eggshells?

In many cases, they are the baby caterpillars' first meal. The shells provide them with the food they need to start growing. Getting rid of their shells has another use. It makes it harder for enemies to find the young caterpillars.

How many body parts do caterpillars have?

The same as adult butterflies and moths—head, thorax, and abdomen. These three main sections are divided into 14 parts, or segments, with joints between them. The joints let the caterpillar bend and move in any direction.

How many legs do caterpillars have?

Three pairs, just like adult moths and butterflies. In addition, most caterpillars have another four or five pairs of short, grasping legs, known as prolegs, on the abdomen. Groups of tiny hooks on the tip of each proleg help the caterpillars cling to leaves and twigs—and to move around.

Can caterpillars see well?

No. The caterpillar's head has six tiny eyes on each side—twelve eyes in all. Even with all these eyes, caterpillars cannot see very well. At best, they can tell light from dark. A few kinds have no eyes at all.

Why do people call caterpillars "eating machines"?

Because they eat and eat and eat. For this job, the caterpillars are equipped with very strong jaws and many teeth. The caterpillar stretches out its head and starts chewing a leaf. When it finishes one leaf, the caterpillar moves on to another.

Caterpillars are always hungry. The more they eat, the more they grow. In one day, some caterpillars gain four or more times their own weight. The polyphemus (pol-uh-FEE-muhs) moth caterpillar holds the record for weight gain. In just the first two days of its life, the caterpillar multiplies its weight 86,000 times!

What do moth caterpillars eat?

The same foods as butterfly caterpillars—loads of green leaves and other plant parts. But unlike other caterpillars, they also dine on wood, hair, and the larvae of other insects. Some moth caterpillars eat animal hair and will nibble wool clothes and blankets.

How does a caterpillar grow bigger?

It grows a new, soft skin under its exoskeleton. Then it sheds the exoskeleton in a process called molting. A caterpillar molts four or five times in its lifetime.

During molting, the old skin on the back of the caterpillar's head splits first. The split then continues down its back. As the exoskeleton becomes loose, the caterpillar pulls itself out. The soft underskin stretches and hardens into the new exoskeleton. Now the caterpillar has room to grow bigger—until the next molt!

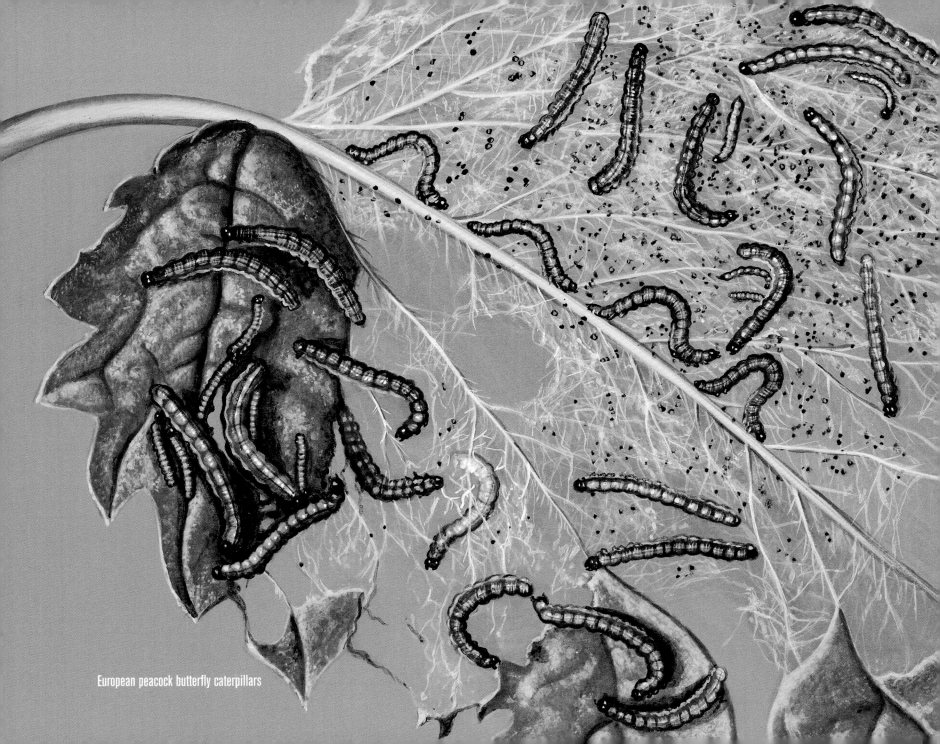

European peacock butterfly caterpillars

European peacock butterfly caterpillars molting

Do caterpillars bite people?

No. But caterpillars do have ways to protect themselves. Some, such as the zebra butterfly, slug moth, and flannel moth caterpillar, have sharp, pointy hairs or bristles that sting like thorns. Other caterpillars have patterns of bright colors. They can be so frightening that they scare enemies away.

The puss moth caterpillar is in a class by itself. It spits acid on any predator that threatens it.

Do caterpillars ever call for help?

Yes. When approached by wasps, many metalmark butterfly caterpillars and some other kinds of caterpillars rub parts of their bodies together. It makes a sound like scraping a comb over the edge of a table.

The call attracts ants, not other caterpillars. The ants come to the rescue and chase away the wasps. As a reward, the caterpillars produce a sweet liquid, known as honeydew, which the ants then feed on. What a treat!

What are inchworms?

Caterpillars of certain kinds of moths and butterflies. These caterpillars make a series of loops as they move. That's why some people call them "loopers." But if you live in the United States, you probably call them inchworms or measuring worms.

How long do caterpillars live?

About a month. After that, most butterfly caterpillars form chrysalises. Most moth caterpillars spin cocoons.

Where does a butterfly caterpillar form its chrysalis?

On a leaf or twig. The caterpillar molts for the last time and stops eating. It squeezes out a sticky liquid from an opening, called a spinneret, below its mouth. Soon the liquid hardens into a pad on the leaf or twig. The caterpillar attaches itself to this pad. Most caterpillars hang upside down. Others spin a silk line, called a girdle, to hold themselves upright.

A hard shell begins to form on the outside. The chrysalis stays very still. But inside, the caterpillar's body slowly changes into an adult butterfly.

Are all butterfly chrysalises alike?

No. Chrysalises have different colors. In some cases, as with the great mormon and common bluebottle, the chrysalises are green or brown. Other chrysalises have a golden glow or bright colors. Those that look like leaves, twigs, or pieces of wood blend in with their surroundings.

The word *chrysalis* comes from the Greek word for gold. Gold spots on some chrysalises help hide them.

BUTTERFLY METAMORPHOSIS

Monarch butterfly caterpillar

Chrysalis

How long does the chrysalis stage last?

From a few days to more than a year. It all depends on the species and the weather. If it's cold, the butterfly may not come out for nine months, or until the weather turns warm and sunny.

How does the adult butterfly emerge?

Through a split in the chrysalis. The legs and antennae come out first. The rest of the wet body follows.

Until it dries out, the butterfly hangs on the empty chrysalis. The insect pumps blood into the veins of its crumpled wings. Gradually the wings straighten out and reach full size. But they're still wet. The butterfly opens and closes them until they are dry and hard. Now the insect is ready to take off. If it is evening, the butterfly rests overnight before flying away.

Emerging butterfly

What is a cocoon?

A covering of silk thread that a moth caterpillar spins around its body. The moth spins enough silk—sometimes as much as ½ mile (0.8 km)—to make the cocoon very thick.

The cocoon covers the moth in the pupa stage, just as the chrysalis protects the butterfly as a pupa. Inside the cocoon, the caterpillar slowly becomes an adult moth.

Are silkworms really worms?

No. Silkworms are the pupae of silkworm moths. Workers, mostly in China and Japan, care for the eggs and caterpillars of these moths on silkworm farms. They feed the caterpillars the leaves of mulberry trees—the caterpillars' only food.

When the pupae finish making their cocoons, workers dip the cocoons in boiling water. This kills the insects and dissolves the substance that holds the silk threads together. Machines then unwind the threads and twist them together to make thicker threads. This silk thread is used to make beautiful silk cloth and clothing.

MOTH METAMORPHOSIS

Silkworm moth caterpillar

Building a cocoon

How much silk thread is in each cocoon?

Very little. It takes about 20,000 cocoons to make 1 pound (500 g) of silk cloth!

How long is it before moths come out of their cocoons?

From a few days to a few months. When the adult moth is ready to emerge, it forces itself out of the cocoon. Like the butterfly, it slowly unfurls its wings and waits for them to dry. Then away it flies.

Do all moths spin cocoons?

No. Some moths dig into the soil or hide under tree bark. But the bodies of all moth pupae, whether in cocoons or not, are covered with a protective shield of a substance known as chitin.

Silkworm moth emerging

STAYING ALIVE

Do butterflies and moths have enemies?

Yes. Hundreds of different kinds of animals eat butterflies and moths. They are special favorites of wasps, bats, birds, frogs, lizards, spiders, and turtles. These animals feed on the butterflies and moths at each stage—egg, caterpillar, chrysalis or cocoon, and adult.

How do butterflies and moths protect themselves?

Camouflage is one way. Different butterflies and moths look like green leaves or dead brown leaves, like tree bark, like twigs or grass—even like bird droppings. Predators have a hard time finding them.

The wings of the Indian leaf butterfly, for example, look exactly like a dead leaf with torn edges. Moldlike spots on the "leaf" help hide the butterfly even more.

Why are some wings different colors underneath?

To confuse the enemy. Consider the red underwing moth, for example. The tops of its wings look like the bark of a willow or poplar tree. But underneath is a bright red band of color. When the moth beats its wings, the bright red flashes. This frightens birds or other foes and gives the moth a chance to escape.

Have any moths changed color over the years?

Yes. Long ago, peppered moths were white with black markings. When resting on light-colored tree trunks, you could hardly see them. Over the last 50 years or so, pollution has darkened many tree trunks. Today, peppered moths are also darker and have more spots.

African hawkmoth

Comma butterfly

Notodontid moth

Indian leaf butterfly

Zebra longwing butterflies

Why do many butterflies have big circles on their wings?

To lead predators to strike at a wing instead of the head. The circles are called eyespots because they look like large eyes. Buckeye butterflies, for example, have big eyespots on their front and back wings. Their enemies often bite here and not the head.

The eyespots sometimes scare foes away. When it rests on a tree in the tropical rain forest, the owl butterfly's large eyespots look like an owl's eyes. A quick glimpse of these large eyespots sends most attackers fleeing.

Which butterflies and moths tend to have bright colors?

Those that taste bad or are poisonous. Predators that bite these insects learn that the bright colors and striking patterns mean trouble. And those that ignore the warning get an awful-tasting mouthful.

Some harmless butterflies keep safe by looking like poisonous butterflies. The orange-and-black monarch butterfly, for example, is poisonous. The almost identical viceroy butterfly is not. Birds that learn to stay away from poisonous monarchs also avoid the harmless viceroys.

How do scales protect butterflies and moths?

They help them escape danger. Suppose a butterfly or moth gets stuck in a spiderweb. As it breaks away, only a few wing scales stick to the web—not the whole wing. The scales pull out as the butterfly or moth flies away safely—only a few scales lighter!

Why do some butterflies smell bad?

To keep safe. Zebra butterflies are an example. Their bad odor is a tip-off to predators to leave them alone. At night, these butterflies sleep together in big, bad-smelling groups.

How does the white ermine moth protect itself?

By playing dead. Many of this moth's enemies will only attack and eat living creatures. So this disguise works very well. If this trick fails, the moth produces a few drops of a smelly yellow liquid. This usually keeps would-be attackers away!

What makes some butterflies and moths taste bad?

Usually the poisonous plants they ate in the caterpillar stage. The caterpillars are not harmed by the poison. But the plants do make the caterpillars and the adults taste terrible.

Spicebush swallowtail butterflies

Why do some butterflies and moths have long tails?

To hide their shape. The tails are on the backs of their wings. This confuses predators, so that they don't attack the insect's body or the main part of its wings. Swallowtail butterflies and luna and comet moths have some of the longest tails of all.

The back wings of the hairstreak butterfly have the same color and shape as its head. Birds generally attack the wrong end of this butterfly!

How long do butterflies live?

Just a few weeks. A small number survive for up to a year. Moths tend to have shorter lives, from a couple of days to several weeks.

As they age, butterfly and moth wings become tattered and torn. By the end of the summer, their colors are less bright. The insects can still fly—but not as well as before.

Bhutan glory butterfly

Where do most butterflies make their homes?

In grasslands and woodlands. You find butterflies in meadows and along the edges of rivers. The meadow brown is a typical grassland butterfly.

Woodland butterflies usually fly at low levels in shady clearings or flutter high among the treetops. The green hairstreak butterfly lives in this woodland setting.

Do butterflies live on mountaintops?

Yes, sometimes. These so-called mountain butterflies must be able to survive difficult weather conditions. They are well suited for short summers, cold nights, and very strong winds. In stormy weather, butterflies fly low and make short flights to avoid being carried away by high winds. At rest, many flatten themselves against rocks and hold on tight to avoid being blown away.

How do mountain butterflies and moths survive?

In various ways. Butterflies that live high in the mountains or in the Arctic are often darker than their lowland cousins. Darker colors soak up more sunlight than light colors, which gives them more energy.

To make the most of the weak Arctic sun, the sooty ringlet butterfly rests on warm rocks. The sun warms its dark wings. Big, hairy scales cover its body and help to hold in the heat. Also, its blood contains a special substance that keeps it from freezing.

Which mountaintop butterfly is most striking?

The peak white butterfly. It lives close to the snows that cover high mountain peaks. Its light color camouflages it against the snow.

Some consider the Bhutan glory even more spectacular. This giant mountain butterfly, with huge eyespots and long tails on its wings, is a sight to remember.

Where do you find the most colorful butterflies and moths?

In the tropics. Here it is warm with lots of rain and there are many different plants and flowers. This makes the tropics an ideal place for butterflies and moths to live.

That's why there are more butterflies in Central and South American rain forests than anywhere else in the world. Swallowtail butterflies are among the largest and most common. Many people say that the blue morpho butterfly is the most beautiful. Others favor the purple emperor butterfly, malachite butterfly, or postman butterfly.

Postman butterfly

Cattle heart swallowtail

Passion vine butterfly

Blue morpho butterfly

Do butterflies and moths live through the winter?

Yes. Many species hibernate, or spend the winter asleep. They hide in tree holes, caves, sheds, or other shelters. Their bodies stop all activity. A special substance in their blood, like antifreeze, helps them survive very low temperatures. When warm weather returns, the butterflies and moths wake up and fly away.

Butterflies and moths can also hibernate as eggs, caterpillars, or pupae. While hibernating, they do not change from one stage to another.

What happens to the butterflies and moths that don't hibernate?

Many die. But some migrate. They form huge groups and fly from a cold place to a warmer place. Butterflies and moths can only fly if the air is warm. So they fly south in the winter and return north in the spring.

Monarch butterflies

Which are the champion migrators?

Monarch butterflies. In late summer or fall, millions of these large fliers gather in flocks in northern parts of America and Canada. They head south in huge swarms, flying as far as 2,500 miles (4,000 km) to California, Florida, or Mexico.

In the spring, the monarchs start their flight back. Along the way, the females stop and lay eggs. Then they die. In time, the eggs hatch. The newborns go through the caterpillar and pupa stages. Then the adults fly back to their summer homes.

How long have butterflies lived on Earth?

About 40 million years. That's the age of the oldest butterfly fossils found so far.

Moths have been around even longer. The first moths lived around the time of the dinosaurs—some 140 million years ago. By the time of the first humans, about 5 million years ago, butterflies and moths were much like those we see today.

Why are butterflies and moths important?

For many reasons. Butterflies are very beautiful. They have been here a long time and are part of our world.

Butterflies and moths carry pollen from flower to flower. When the butterflies or moths drink nectar from a flower, some pollen sticks to their bodies. Then, as they visit other flowers, the pollen drops off. Many plants need pollen to produce fruit and seeds and start new plants.

Lepidoptera are important, too, because of the huge number of them eaten by other animals. Centipedes, spiders, and many groups of insects prey on them. Frogs, toads and lizards, small rodents, bats, and monkeys eat them, too. Even people in some countries gulp down caterpillars—fried and crunchy.

Will butterflies and moths live forever on planet Earth?

We hope so. In some countries, butterflies are disappearing because people are moving into their habitats. There is much we can do to protect these beautiful creatures. If you have a garden, you can plant flowers to attract butterflies by day and moths at night. Choose plants, like thistles, yarrow, and goldenrod, that will feed caterpillars and butterflies. Try not to disturb these insects at any stage of their development. In the summer, you'll see caterpillars eating leaves, moths resting in the tree bark, and butterflies sunning themselves on flowers. If everyone helps, butterflies and moths may live forever on planet Earth.

Banana eater

INDEX

About the Authors

The Bergers are concerned about the loss of butterfly habitats due to the construction of buildings, roads, and other projects. One way they try to help butterflies survive is by growing black-eyed Susans, bee balm, yarrow, goldenrod, daisies, and other flowers that attract and feed butterflies.

About the Illustrator

Higgins Bond has illustrated many books about nature and animals. She recently illustrated four stamps depicting endangered species for the United Nations Postal Service.